The Life of a Dolphin

Branca Tani

Rosen REAL READERS

Rosen Classroom™
New York

Dolphins live in oceans.

Dolphins swim together.

Dolphins eat fish.

Dolphins jump.

Dolphins are friendly.

Dolphins like to play.

Words To Know

dolphin

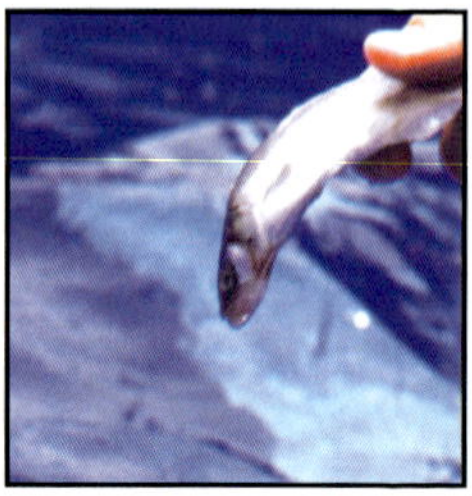

fish

ocean